## See for Yourself

# Trees

## See for Yourself

# Trees

Karen Bryant-Mole
Photographs by Barrie Watts

RSVP
RAINTREE
STECK-VAUGHN
PUBLISHERS
The Steck-Vaughn Company

*Austin, Texas*

Published by Raintree Steck-Vaughn Publishers, an imprint of Steck-Vaughn Company

Editor: Kathy DeVico
Project Manager: Lyda Guz
Electronic Production: Scott Melcer

All photographs by Barrie Watts except: p. 9 Laurie Campbell/NHPA; p. 11 Martin Garwood/NHPA; p. 14 John Clegg/Ardea London; p. 23 Stephen Dalton/NHPA; p. 27 Lady Philippa Scott/NHPA.

**Library of Congress Cataloging-in-Publication Data**
Bryant-Mole, Karen.
    Trees / Karen Bryant-Mole; photographs by Barrie Watts.
      p.    cm. — (See for yourself)
    Includes index.
    ISBN 0-8172-4212-0
    1. Trees—Juvenile literature.   [1. Trees.]   I. Watts, Barrie, ill.
II. Title.   III. Series.
QK475.8.B78   1996
582.16—dc20                       95-31131
                                       CIP
                                       AC

Printed and bound in the United States
1 2 3 4 5 6 7 8 9 0  99 98 97 96 95

# Contents

# Where Do Trees Grow?

There are lots of trees in the countryside.
A big group of trees is called woods, or a forest.
You can see part of some woods in the big picture.

Trees grow in towns, too. You can see them planted
along the sides of roads, in yards, and in parks.

You could draw a picture of
a tree growing in a park or
in your school playground.
(Take an adult with you
to the park.)

Trees come in all shapes
and sizes.
Some are tall and thin.
Others are round and bushy.

What sort of shape does
your tree make?

# Tree Parts

The big stalk, or stem, of a tree is called the trunk.
A tree's trunk has a special covering to protect it.
This covering is called bark.

Look closely at the big picture.
The bark on the tree looks cracked and broken.
As the tree grows bigger, the bark on the outside
stretches and cracks. But underneath the old bark,
new bark is growing.

Trees usually have lots of branches.
Branches grow outward
from the trunk.
Smaller branches, called twigs,
sprout from the main branches.

All trees grow leaves.
Their leaves grow from
buds on the twigs.
This picture is of a twig.
Can you see its bud?

8

# Different Trees, Different Names

Do you know what kind of tree this is?
It is called a wild cherry tree.

Looking closely at a tree will help you find out
what kind of tree it is. There are lots of clues to help you.

First, look at its bark. Is it rough or smooth?
This cherry tree has smooth, reddish-brown bark.

What shape are the tree's leaves?
Pick one leaf. Is its shape long or oval?
Are there lots of leaves on one stalk?
Does the leaf have points, or does it
have rounded edges?

Once you know what the leaves and
the bark of the tree look like, you can
find out what kind of tree it is by
looking in a book about trees.

Press your leaf into some modeling clay.
Keep the clay as a record of the
leaf's shape.

10

# Why Trees Need Water

Trees have roots, which grow down into the ground.
Look closely at the bottoms of these trees.
You will see some fingerlike shapes that
disappear into the ground.
These are the tops of the trees' roots.

The roots of the trees take in water from the soil.
Trees need lots of water.
A tree's roots usually spread out a long way.
This is so they can find as much water as possible.

The water travels up
tubes in the trunk to
the tree's leaves.

This picture shows
part of a leaf.
The lines on the leaf are
tiny tubes, called veins.
The veins carry water
to all parts of the leaf.

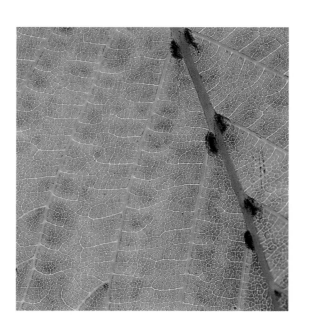

12

# Food for Trees

The tree's green leaves use water, air, and sunlight to make food for the tree.

The water comes up to the leaves through the roots, trunk, and branches. The branches of the tree spread out so that the leaves can get as much sunlight and air as possible.

This photograph is part of the underside of a leaf. It was taken through a microscope. The microscope makes the leaf look much bigger than it really is.

Can you see the holes on it? These holes are called stomata.
They let air in and out.
They let water out, too.

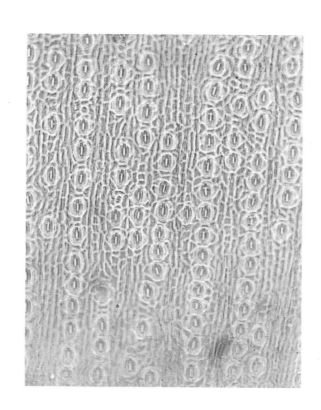

# Losing Leaves

Look at the big picture. It was taken in the fall.
The leaves on these beech trees have changed color.
Some of the leaves have fallen to the ground.
In the winter, the branches of the trees will be bare.

Trees that lose their leaves in the fall are
called deciduous trees.

Some trees have leaves all year round.
They are called evergreen trees.
Most evergreen trees have long, needlelike leaves.
These leaves have a waxy coating. It protects them
during the cold weather. In the winter, the
leaves on these fir trees stay green and shiny.

# Fruit and Flowers

Trees usually flower in the spring or early summer.
The flowers make a yellow powder, called pollen.
The pollen is carried from one flower to another.
This is called pollination.

Some trees are pollinated by insects.
Insects carry the pollen on their bodies.
The bee in the big picture is on an apple tree flower.

Other trees are pollinated by the wind,
which blows the pollen from
one flower to another.

After pollination occurs, the tree's
flowers die, and its fruit starts to grow.
Seeds grow inside of the fruit.
Ask a grown-up to help
you cut an apple in half.
How many seeds can
you find inside?

# Seeds Bring New Life

This apple (pictured right) has fallen off the tree.
The fruit is starting to rot.
As it rots, some of its seeds will fall onto the soil.
New trees may start to grow from these seeds.

Apple trees have soft fruit. Some trees, like the oak
tree, have hard fruit. Its fruit are called acorns.

You can grow your own tree from a seed.
Stick four toothpicks into the
sides of an avocado seed.
Fill an empty jelly jar with water.
Balance the seed so that it just
touches the water. Wait for the
seed to grow roots.

When the roots are about as long
as your finger, you can plant
your young tree in some soil.
Keep your tree indoors.

# Trees Have Long Lives

The oak tree in the big picture is more than a hundred years old. Some kinds of trees can live for thousands of years!

You can figure out roughly how old some types of trees are. Sycamores, oaks, chestnuts, and flowering cherries are good trees to use.

Every year, a tree's trunk grows by about an inch (3 cm) around its middle. So a tree that measures about 10 inches (30 cm) around its trunk must be about ten years old.

Find a big tree that is standing by itself. Measure around its trunk. How old is your tree?

# Home for Many

Can you find the entrance to the woodpecker's nest in this picture? Woodpeckers make holes in the trunks of trees by pecking at the bark with their beaks.

Many insects make their homes in trees, too. Caterpillars and leaf miners eat the leaves of trees. Millipedes and wood lice live in the bark.

You can catch some of these small insects in a tree trap. Ask an adult to help you cut the end off a plastic bottle. Turn the end around, and put it back into the bottle. Hang your tree trap from a branch outside.

Go back the next day. What is inside? Remember to release any insects after you have looked at them.

# How Trees Help Us

Here is a picture of some lemon trees.

We use trees in lots of different ways. We can pick fruit and nuts from trees. How many different kinds of fruit and nuts can you think of? We can even make medicines from some trees.

Wood comes from trees. Furniture is often made from wood. Wood is also used to make paper.

You could make a collection of things that have been made from wood.

Now you know how useful trees are, and why we must take care of them.

When trees are cut down for their wood, new trees should be planted to take their places.

# More Things to Do

**1.** Make a leaf rubbing.
Put a piece of paper on top of a dry leaf.
Rub a crayon gently over the paper.
Your leaf should appear, as if by magic.
Can you see the leaf's veins on your rubbing?

**2.** Keep a tree diary.
Choose a tree that grows in your yard or in your school playground. Study your tree, and draw a picture of it. Which birds and insects visit your tree? Notice how your tree changes from one season to the next.

**3.** Tree sayings
Can you figure out what these sayings mean?

   To be unable to see the woods for the trees.
   To be at the top of the tree.
   From little acorns, mighty oak trees grow.
   To be rooted to the ground.

**4.** Find some tree rings.
Each year a tree's trunk grows a new ring of wood. Look at some wooden furniture. Can you see lines and loops on it? These are part of the tree trunk's rings. Sometimes you can see dark spots, too. These are called knots. They show where branches once sprouted from the tree's trunk.

# Index

This index will help you find some
of the important words in this book.

# Notes for Parents and Teachers

These notes will give you some additional information about trees and suggest some more activities you might like to try with children.

## Pages 8–9

A tree is a woody plant whose trunk and main branches get bigger every year. The difference between a tree and a shrub is that a tree only has one main stem (its trunk), whereas a shrub has several stems growing from the ground.

## Pages 12–15

Photosynthesis is the process by which green plants make food for themselves. Chlorophyll in the green leaves captures the energy in sunlight. This energy is used to turn water (that has been brought to the leaves from the tree's roots in the soil) and carbon dioxide into oxygen and carbohydrates. Trees can only photosynthesize during the day, because they need sunlight in order to do so.

Trees breathe in oxygen and breathe out carbon dioxide. They breathe through tiny holes in their leaves. These tiny holes are called stomata. Trees also lose water vapor through their stomata. The loss of water vapor through the stomata is called transpiration. The transpiration stream is the process in which water is drawn up through the roots of the tree and lost through its leaves, thereby causing the tree to draw up more water through its roots.

## Pages 16–17

Although evergreen trees do not lose all of their leaves in the winter, as deciduous trees do, their leaves do eventually turn brown and drop off. The difference is that the leaves on evergreen trees do not all drop off at the same time. The veins in the leaves of deciduous trees spread out in a fan shape (see page 12). The veins in evergreen leaves are usually arranged in parallel lines.

## Pages 18–19

Fruit comes in many shapes and sizes. Children could be encouraged to investigate this. The fruit of the horse chestnut tree is the prickly, outer casing that protects its seed. Its seed is the conker. The fruit of a conifer tree is usually a woody cone. When the seeds are ripe, the scales of the cone open up, and the seeds drop out.

## Pages 22–23

Every year a tree's trunk grows a new ring of wood. This is called an annual ring. It means that, year by year, the circumference of the tree's trunk gets bigger. This is the principle behind the activity on page 22. The rule of thumb of one inch per year is most accurate for particular varieties of trees that grow in open spaces, and are between fifteen and one hundred years old. The rings on trees that are older than this will become very narrow and make the calculation less accurate. It is possible to figure out the exact age of a felled tree by counting the rings on its stump.